THE GROUND

FARRAR STRAUS GIROUX   NEW YORK

THE

ROWAN RICARDO PHILLIPS

GROUND

FARRAR, STRAUS AND GIROUX

18 West 18th Street, New York 10011

Copyright © 2012 by Rowan Ricardo Phillips

All rights reserved

Distributed in Canada by D&M Publishers, Inc.

Printed in the United States of America

First edition, 2012

Library of Congress Cataloging-in-Publication Data

Phillips, Rowan Ricardo.

The ground : poems / Rowan Ricardo Phillips. — 1st ed.

p. cm.

ISBN 978-0-374-16708-0 (alk. paper)

I. Title.

PS3616.H467 G76 2012

811'.6—dc23

2011040612

Designed by Quemadura

www.fsgbooks.com

1 3 5 7 9 10 8 6 4 2

FOR NÚRIA AND IMOGEN

*Where wast thou when I laid the
foundations of the earth? . . .
When the morning starres sang
together, and all the sonnes
of God shouted for joy?*

—JOB 38:4-7

CONTENTS

THE GROUND

TONIGHT

In the beginning was this surface. A wall. A beginning.

Tonight it coaxed music from a Harlem cloudbank. It freestyled

A smoke from a stranger's coat. It stole thinned gin.

It was at the edge of its beginnings but outside

Looking in. The lapse-blue facade of Harlem Hospital is
weatherstill

Like a starlit lake in the midst of Lenox Avenue.

Tonight I touched the tattooed skin of the building I was born in

And because tonight is curing the beginning let me through.

And everywhere was blurring halogen. Love the place that
welcomed you.

SONG OF FULTON AND GOLD

The eye seeking home
has to lower
        lower
           lower

lower. The eye seeking
home has to
lower.

*

The eye seeking home
has to lower
        lower
           lower

lower. The eye seeking
home has to
lower.

*

The eye seeking home
has to lower
               lower

                    lower

lower. The eye seeking
home has to
lower.

                    *

The eye seeking home
has to lower
               lower

                    lower

lower. The eye seeking
home has to
lower.

                    *

There are no
towers.

TERRA INCOGNITA

I plugged my poem into a manhole cover
That flamed into the first guitar,
Jarred the asphalt and tar to ash,
And made from where there once was
Ground a sound instead to stand on.

TABULA RASA

Tell me now, Poem, if you know: In the end when I'm gone,
  will you go, too?
Are you your possible answer? Would you tell me the truth if
  you knew?
Do you have something for me? Is everything a maybe with
  you? Does
Maybe not matter when maybe's a landscape of untethered
  starlight?
Is maybe is? Do you need to repeat how, explain why,
Explain how and why you repeat? Are you what's gold in the
  mind's gray-green
Weather? The verdigris of hexameters trailing dawn copters?
Scarce sounds scissoring through darkness? Or simply the
  darkness itself?

A VISION THROUGH THE SMOKE

A tree half aflame moaned inside me.
The willow that had wept would not weep.
All of me, the pigeons cry, *all of me*
Or is it *allofyou allofyou* that they coo?
The skyline held the sun up like two carnival strongmen
But then seemed to drop with the greatest of ease.
No I I knew could clear the clouding mirror:
Not the sun as it set nor the moon as it bruised.

GOLDEN

For once, I slept and you watched.
I dreamed, I think.
I washed without my hands.

You watched. I moved along a scratchy plain
Of dandelion, peony, wild
And luckless clover. A bee entered me.

You soothed my ache. We watched a golden sky
Heckled into slate.
I will wake and say, "Golden." I will wake

And say, no, nothing but that. I had become
The injurer who makes things golden,
Swimming in your voice, so much deeper than mine.

EMBRACE THE NIGHT AND GET THEE GONE

Talking picture. Silent poem.
New York shakes off the fall.
Tonight
I work in a silence
That prays the rare turn to sound.
I make nothing. I am fractured.
I walk in the dark egg of
Another September night
That is cool, that is
Cool as though the moon is a mouth
That blows on its wound.
We are early in the life of the poet.
He knows so little of light,
So little of shadow. He knows down
Town as a metaphor. He knows
The constellations are at work tonight
Whoring their stories of strife.
He's in search of life. A poem's
In search of its body. Down
Toward the river

The skyline
Broaches its phalanx of broken teeth.
And up above in the grounded sky the sky grinds down the stars.

And up above in the grounded sky the sky grinds down. The stars
Broach its phalanx of broken teeth.
The skyline
Toward the river
Searches for its body: downed,
Dammed up, beached; like the end of a poem
Walled up against competitive life.
The constellations are at work tonight.
Betelgeuse. Bellatrix. The hunter's bow
In elegy graffitied across the endless black gate.
We know so little of light:
It dies though we are early in its life.
A beautiful night. Its lambent moon
Lets down a light that only happens in September.
Say it. *September.* Fragile
As an egg now. Teetering. Parabolic.
Broken teeth in the mouth
That prays the rare turn to sound.
I work through the silence.

Tonight
New York shakes off the fall.
Silent poem. Talking picture.

Embrace the night and get thee gone.

MAP, INCOMPLETE, 1665

It's his vision of this piss-colored parchment.
With griffins cinched near the edges of the frame.
As Africa, newly rivered, sits mysterious as the brain
Of his New World, its synopsis as curt as

Enjambment. Its proposed longitudes and latitudes
Meeting mid-ocean and forming warped crosses
Wrapping around the water and blunted by these bulges
In which Heaven, Earth, and Author spell themselves out in
    perfect Latin.

At night, or at day (whichever his diary will say),
A Dutch cartographer dreams, head dragging
Down on his desk, of Uccello's *Saint George and the Dragon*.
How, in that flat world of triangle, circle, and square

The world seemed so eager to summarize itself:
Woman timed by rescue; man trapped in that stout,
Conning hourglass; a two-legged monster spit out
From a cave in a pose so wretched he wakes to trace it

As out his window the soft prismatic Dutch light
Slowly traces its rising lover, New York.

PROPER NAMES IN THE

LYRICS OF TROUBADOURS

My parents never call me Rowan.
I'm Ricky, from Ricardo.
But not Ricky Ricardo.

I'm also the first Phillips in my family.
My mother decided Phillip, my father's
Family name, sounded too much like a first name

(In America, at least).
Rowan Phillip would lead inevitably
To Phillip Rowan. That was her story, and she's sticking to it.

For the record, that's an Old Norse first name,
A Spanish middle name,
And one of those faux-English-faux-Dutch-sounding last names

That's really Greek for lover of horses.
"Rowan Ricardo Phillips":
Another of those names that straddles seas in the sails of unseen

Ships. Still, it sounds typically West Indian to me.
And like "the West Indies" indefinite.
An indefinite noun in an indefinite poem.

It took me a while to accept it.

MARE INCOGNITUM

That I can't recall my first glimpse of my mother:
Alien-eyed, wrapped in alien cloth, how could
I? Once she held me she just was my mother,

That's just how it goes. This is just one of many
Beautiful moments I've been a part of but can't
(And won't ever) remember. That's just life, I guess.

The void. That's just a part of life: some hidden cave
Sunk deep in the mind and built for Beautiful But
Can't Remember. I saw it once: here dissolving,

There reassembling like gleaned second-long seasons.
And for what reason? I just don't know. Years asking
Myself Why? Why can we not remember this? passed.

Are we here because the mere dust of stars torched
In the throat of an equation? It's a cold thought,
I know. But belief just burns brighter in the cold,

Brighter as the first idea flares and reverses
Like the first new motion of that first majestic
Ocean just as it discovered impregnable ground.

MUSIC FOR WHEN

THE MUSIC IS OVER

In the beginning: no beginning—
For once we were the void and nothing else.
There were no starfields but this one starfield
Where the first star fumed and ate its own heart.

We were that star until ourselves and then.
And then a marigold, a man in gold,
The sublimities art gives a throat to.
How even bitter, garroted Saturn

Half listens as he hangs in space, barely
Himself, his moons tending to him like flies
To a corpse. We live like the one sequin
In a sequined dress that thinks it's the dress

Although it merely blurs from other lights
Ablaze and bending. Look up, love. Listen.
We are the world and what's wrong with the world
Is what the birds grow tired of singing.

TO THE READER

If you want to talk to me you'll send me
An email. If you don't know my email
You can Google it. If that's not enough

You can pay a site for all my info
And then use Google Maps to find my street.
My building's the blue one but please don't come

By; I think we've got a good thing going
Here: we both thrive on a type of moving
Silence like that sound you hear in static

And just know is something more than static
So you lean in and start to feel something
Tighten and crack like frightened wings on fire

That dwindle down to your lap like a cat.
Hi, I'm Rowan. We likely haven't met.
And if we have or have not I love you.

ABINGDON SQUARE PARK

I once had had a thought
About a thought I once had had

About whether it was natural
For nature to seem so natural,

Whether there was a Man in the Sun
Who steadied the sun with levers,

Pulleys, and gears, and if so whether
He ever managed not to be there,

Whether we gauge and are gauged
By what randomly remains

As the bang implodes back
Into the calyx of its heart

And singes and sings and searches
For itself in the intersperséd dark.

I once had had a thought.
I was here in Abingdon Square Park.

There were these magnificent Technicolor
Tulips. Their tips were tilted like blind lips.

They sang like heralds of the spring.
And by June they were gone.

HERALDS OF DELICIOSO COCO HELADO

FOR ROLAND BURNS

The moods of the cantaloupe king are moods
Of the melon king in green variations.
Both entered the orange parlor like nations
Seeking peace from their wintered wars in the woods.

Both entered the parlor to say goodbye
Or farewell or peace or adios, ciao,
Adieu, or tschüß; however the ground
Seals its truce. But the old interpreter just sighed.

The old interpreter would not speak—
And instead sighed those winters like a spout,
Drowning the parlor with what he spat out
Until the parlor broke in half at grief's peak

And the kings could taste as they fell through the snow
Delicioso coco helado.

GRIEF AND THE IMAGINARY GRAVE

November snowfall drowns out views
Of Grand, Summit, and Story Avenues.

Gone gone gonegonegone I choked
On the thought of ending this song.

Three Bronx streets go down under snow
That grays in the air like aging hair.

Understoried. Dead and buried. Do you
Hear me from where they buried you?

From where they buried you do you
Hear the rhyme I bury for you?

Do you age in an orbit of perfect
Sunshine and sound?

Gone gone gone gone all I can say is gone.
Because gone is what is here

Among the other things that grow.

MAPPA MUNDI

These factories, their pipes' smoke, plume like skunks,
Rise as one and few and many and all
And forty fireflies bound for JFK.

Forty more circle where here be dragons.
Nature is a lapse in city life.
Whether red birds sit and sing from rooftops

Or rappers cipher deep into the night,
The gun-in-your-mouth talk of a ransomed
God, nature is a lapse in city life.

The soft green ground that ends an avenue.
The red rust-spew stifling a drain.
Pigeon-dropped icicles. Nature is a lapse in city life.

Those kids on a New Deal rooftop
Staring at the wonders of Moses,
Who with a wave split the Bronx asunder

And dropped the Cross Bronx
Down in his wake,
May they know this map of the world

As only a map of the world.
One of many that will lead them
To and from their doors.

BIRD OF FIRE

E il suo

volo di fuoco m'accecò sull'altro

The blurred moon, blanched in the new evening sky,
Amazed me as a child. How could it live
At the same time as the sun (Downstar
I called it), captured by the melody
That rang out from it, dusk-bright, like a phoenix
Downed in civil twilight. The difference

Between the two, I thought, was difference
Itself: it made things real. But is the sky
Real? Aren't its blue moments, like the phoenix,
Just the mind's conjugations of "to live,"
Or the brain's long division of "to die"?
Rouge le soir, bel espoir, sings the Downstar

Down night's starry throat, already elsewhere, Downstar
No more, no longer the sweet difference
Between real and dream I knew. I will die.
I am not a dream. I am not quite real.
I am a dream's firm ground. And I live
Because they are not what I am. Keep this

Thought for me, Poetry, as the phoenix
Seduces dreadnoughts to strum the Downstar
To sleep, and the skyline's lights begin to live
Like notes in air; and in that difference,
That sleight of sun, may night remake the torqued sky
And distill dream and real from live and die.

A red cloud, speckled like an amorphous die,
Ferries the Internet's dead. "Off to Phoenix!";
"TGIF!"; "Double Rainbow!"; "Nice sky
Tonight!"; "Don't let this get you down, Starr."
They speak, spammed or hacked, the indifference
In that act excused in saying, "A guy's got to live."

I chased the verb with the bird that always lives,
Saddled on its nape as it dove to die,
Its neck arched to the moon. Indifference
Spread through its ash-blond body now phoenix
No more, now part of the ground, now downed star.
Its frame, first feathered by flames, flailed blue. Sky

Swallowed the phoenix, seized round the Downstar,
Sang sky down to the city, burned livid
Until it didn't, then praised the difference.

AS THE HEART OF THE SUN

DESCENDS ON TRIBECA

As a glean of orange cream glazed the dark and glowing calm
And everything that goes away has gone,

I wait for you on North Moore Street within the sun's
    imagination,
The wind fretting the lofts, the moon rising behind me.

The world is a tossed-out sketch dug up to be used again.
The world is a crumpled paper found and flattened out.

And in the creases of its ground a supple world stares
Back; the roofless amanuensis, all scribbled song and dares.

I'll show you mine if you show me yours
And all the real world will be ours
Even though you are not here and I'm still miles away.

TWO TWILIGHTS

Summer. And the sinking lights of summer.
And the sinking city lights of summer
Dancing down the long hips of the Hudson.

Dancing down the long hips of the Hudson.
Shrinking, enchanting with outrageous calm.
Until from just under, wood pikes peek out:

First like goose bumps, then like bones through skin.
Look down: MORTON STREET, carved into the ground.
And these stumps, tricked out with seagull scarecrows,

Still wait here for their ship: like that wet bruise
Lake Avernus still waits for Dante's soul,
Checking the reflection of every star

Trapped in its dim circles, and whispering
Per me si va ne la città dolente
To see if, from the memory, one flinches.

PURGATORIO, XXVI: 135–148

Ieu sui Arnaut, que plor e vau cantan

He was gone. Like a leap

Of flame that, after having burst from the sun,
   Is dragged back into the sun as though nothing,
   Leaving only the seen surface of the sun.

I'd lost my way. I had no guide but a light:
   The slowly approaching twilight. And I said,
   "Light be this world," and I said, "World this be Light."

And slowly a bright starfield fell to the sea,
   Fell all about the one my guide had pointed out.
   And he said, *Rastaman. Higher man. Angel*

Seven-sealed . . . No. But I smell some of the smoke
   Of Babylon on I. Come closer. Closer.
   So I-man ave some ital veneration.

I am Bob, who weep and strum and gather and
   Love all tings lickle and small. Jah left I lung
   And guitar to sing to everyone. All dem!

But I nah know ting bout dem but what I sing.
  And I nah wan know ting. I nah wan know ting!
  So when I complete I uphill trip to I

Sing some of I soul you see ere so close peeled
  From I-man structure. Sing some of dread in I
  So I&I don't find it so easy love Bob dead.

Then he fled as the lion that defined him.

THE LONG SLOW GOODBYE

The river nods off. The Dog Star digs in.
All sumptuous glimpse of nothingness, like nothing
Firm in fog. A tree half aflame grows inside me.
Its flames put out by its green, then lit again
By everything that that green has been.
In another life I hid my poems from serious in Sirius,
Tucked them in the white-hot mind supplied the distant star . . .
So that when the years destroy me, or worse, the muse
Just leaves, I'll at least have left you something, faint but in the blood,
Like what Dionysus' one disciple who did not tear his flesh
Discovered as she heard the head of Orpheus singing her name.

THE GREENNESS OF THE GROUND

The Lord, whose name is Jealous, is a jealous god.
Green-gripped, who dripped the moon half eaten, jaded mud
    and char.
With any flourish or flame there came terror. The dog
Died eyeing Heaven. The city, not yet torched, saw no change,
No sudden clarity until came down *I am the Lord, that*
Is my name; I will not give my glory to another.
Then, among everything everywhere alight inviting endlessly
    unmaking and making,
I will be Jealous for my Holy name. And while
Kneeling there we buried the hound. The sea stayed jade.
    We prayed.

A MEDITATION ON MANY

THINGS OUT OF MY CONTROL

I grew so tired of doing little, but
I did little more. And from my mores grew
Everything: the horizon, night, a light
Cramped and scattered like blackbirds from a wire
That leave behind nothing, not even the
Wire, not even the six evenings of God
And God's work, not even the sky-scuffed sea;
Which was north, south, present, past, and future;
Which cracked oil tankers like eggs of speckled
Steel; all just to spite this plain shore who'd said
She was just as beautiful as the moon,
Beautiful as the moon who now smears her.

GRIEF AND THE IMAGINARY

GRAVE, VOL. 2: RED TRILLIUM

Headstone shoots up
Like a cartrunk
Sunk in the seabed

Headstone shoots up
Like a cartrunk
Sunk in the seabed

Drank so much wine
Flowers grow round his grave
Cherry red

Drank so much wine
Flowers grow round his grave
Cherry red

Drink sunk his car like junk
You can't get out
Your head

Said

Drink sunk his car like junk
You just
Can't get out your head

Drank so much wine
Flowers flame up from his grave
Cherry red

Drank so much wine flowers flame
Up from his grave deep
Cherry red

Wake-robin
Stinking Benjamin
Red trillium

Wildflower lives
For wildflower dead

OVER THE COUNTIES OF KINGS AND QUEENS CAME THE SECOND IDEA

After a long night swimming
In the dry dark of a book
I heard outside my window
A sound that changed my window.

Each of the planets unseen sang
As though in the grooves
Of a record I loved.
Saturn, Jupiter, Venus, Mars,

A scratch where the Earth
Where the Earth should be
Where the Earth should be
And is.

I stared out into the darkness
For some sign of the cold consoler,
That perched spinning
Night nurse who tends

To the sleeping sun
Destined to rise irresponsibly
Over the counties
Of Kings and Queens.

What are we during these
Archaic moments
Of mind-made Shangri-la
But bees trapped in amber,

Storyless and beheld,
By the amber god
Who makes it so
And the living god

Who undoes it?

APOCALYPSE WITH SASQUATCH

No one left. No one left but chum for the zombies
Under a skyline spotted with climbing Sasquatch, haddock,
    starling, roach.
All railing, all life derailed under the cracked and fulvous moon.
New York is six chandeliers spiked to the ground,
Its buildings licked clean by the aardvark's tongue of fire.
And nothing now is apocrypha. Nothing confuses. No one's left.
    No one
Left to tell me Hell is a stalking elsewhere,
Or Hell is other people, or I myself am Hell.
For Hell is what's sufficient to the notion that you still live
And make from where there once was nothing
Something worse far worse than you.
So said the Sasquatch from the last penthouse window
Of the crumbling co-op facing flowering Abingdon Square.

TWO PRELUDES

I

We were made to forget and nothing else.
Or, we forget until there's nothing else.
Or, nothing else forgets us but ourselves.
We are here for this and this alone
And give back to the hushed scattered starlight
Pulsing each of our names into the near,
Imperceptible, inaudible void.
The first margin, that inaugural depth
That casts its clean and cosmic reflection
Down into these ditches we call seas, stirs,
And, in simply being, shall always be . . .
Whether in us, for ourselves, in this world,
Or, as a relation of Disorder,
Who forgot what it was so long ago
That it relates disorder with us,
And makes its unimaginable thing:
You as you are now and you as you shall be.

II

We were made to forget and little else.
Or, we forget until there's little else.
Or, little else forgets us but ourselves.
We're here now. Not much more is given.
And even this demands some reliance
On religion, perception, and science.
Tonight the first horizon returns and
Casts down into sleeping conchs the song of
First light. Will you hear it? Few things live
In us that really remain part of us
Apart from the diaphanous and strange;
How, one day, when we're completely forgotten
In incalculable clouds of cloudless ore
Its core will cheer what it there imagines:
This as it was and this as it shall be.

SONNET 3.0

There is no singing of her   though I sing
Of her   This is always a bad idea
But these   are the habits of the poets
The   old habits I've picked up   peeling love
From blank pages   -   and love   from letters
Undulating their cold feathers   above
The sunk red line   of the slowly   rising
Night   There is no singing   of her   She is
Not a habit of the brain   She is real
And   as with all things real   some sealed
    chance   sounds
Inside her   An insight of her   hers   alone
To know alone   and prosperous of   Fill in the Blank
    Create
A Username   Set a Password   Enter
Enter   Enter   Enter   Try Again   or
    Restart

EURYDICE

She folded back,
Folded back, folded
Back . . .

Like a letter
You plan
To keep.

The content to memory.
The tone
To heart.

The envelope
Slashed open
And impossible

To repair.

THE DOUBLE DEATH OF ORPHEUS

Somewhere she's repeeling apples,
Repeeling apples and pinning them up again,
Pinning them up again in their trees.

They had nothing to do with Hell
And everything to do with Hell.
He thought he'd find her in Hell

When she was actually interning in Heaven.
She worked in all the departments there:
Cloudkeeping, Front Desk, Reservations.

The attempt on Heaven and its loss
Of innocence made Heaven seem
Less seedy. She loved sometimes

To pick an apple straight from the tree on her
Break. This was encouraged there:
The good being encouraged to listen to their impulses,

Carpe diem, etc. She'd move the blade across
The round red surface of the fruit
Like a sail navigating through a Hell-spawned

Sea as the sun dropped down to drink it.
She turnered both the apple she turned
And the turning slaver in his heart.

He grew consumed with little things like this
The second time he lost her. The first time
Even gravity gave in as he descended the Earth

To find her. But then not even the power
Of his strum shaking the ground
Could stir him.

To bring her back, don't look back.
It was more counsel than condition: *To bring her back, don't*
Look back. Hell loves to be taken literally.

But could you blame him?
Were there even double meanings back then
When everything was meaning something

For the first time? Maybe his art
Just fooled his heart;
Or maybe his screwed-up heart

Just screwed up;
Either way,
He was done;

His heart split and spun
Like that ridiculous compass
In Donne,

And he'd never do her again.

REVERSE ORPHEUS

And saw his own death happen.
But as a mending this time, a cleaning.
They shoved his limbs together,

Flailed off all the blood,
Then dimmed into the distance
Like the dots of an ellipsis.

The shattered boulders rebounded,
Rolled back up their ruts.
The sea's sea-lathered sun

Succumbed in the wrong direction.
Soon the joy of Life Returned
Returned his strange thin smile

But it sunk into a frown
And then the Saddest Song of All.
This is how it started.

He was back where he'd parted.

REVERSE EURYDICE

Damaged he fell through mountains to find her.
Down there among some thirty-three headstones
And countless unmarked plots: Eurydice.

He climbed back up the cliff. Patted the earth.
Shoveled her out. Pulled the coin from her tongue.
Acceptance. Depression. Deal-making. Rage.

Denied, he denied it all. She awoke
Again all amber in an amber field
Where she's just been bitten by a trampled

Snake, the poison draining from her soft long
Tender calf back to the sacks of its source.
She's midway to the meadow she's in now.

Now she's home. Now she's marrying. Now she's
Meeting him for the first time. "Hi, my name
Is Orpheus," he says. Then he doesn't.

APOLLO: SEASON THREE

In the span of a summer I grew half a foot.
My feet grew, too. My mind learned delicious.
The ground leaned against a deciduous forest.
First I called it tree. Then I called it delicious.
Delicious said, "Tell Shaggy, Fred, Thelma, and Scoob
To come find me. My name is Daphne."
But I broke Daphne's arm instead.
It was a cruelty I first tried to blame on nature.
Then on growing up, on falling off, on it being
Just an old myth. But the world would have none of it
And canceled me after season three.
Say it straight, say it straight, the crickets chanted.
Change your name, change your name, the arroba urged.
But the great god of poetry was at a loss for words
And fell back into his habit of speaking in the third person.
He's always trended more accessible this way.

AUGUST IN FATIGUES

The war flaws every summer night
Like the clouds in her precious stone.

LEAKS

Out of the city he's loathed. So it's highly unlikely a shave and a
    haircut
Make the agenda for this trip: if we cancel the hit, though, our
    Plan B
Must and I mean must work—understand? And we still have to
    pay the
Barber. See? That's why I told Payroll we should have paid him up
    front.
Payroll getting involved was, is, and will probably always
Be (in my mind) a tremendously dangerous error on our part.

*

Send me a text with some poems. If our guy is right, then I'll
    need some poems.

*

Singing about light in lamps? By the end of the night I gave up
Hope of him signing the deal. He just wouldn't stop; so I smiled
    through it.

*

Please don't send more poems. Not intended to sound quite that
    harsh but
Will trust you know what I mean. And whatever you do: please
    delete these.

*

Absolute chaos now. Saw the Tunisian, Mohammed, douse oil
Over his head. That the government would have presumed that
    this too
Would pass, good God, what were they thinking. We'll need Plan
C if this spreads; and I'll have to repatriate: too soon.

COPPER HORSE

Ten dollars for two nights:
Sweden to St. Petersburg.

I crossed the Baltic Sea
Fueled on toffee and warm beer,

Refuged in a Russian disco room
As red as it was dark,

Where no one spoke
But Dolly Parton

Bent like a fleur-de-lis
Across the face

Of a broken Bally
Pinball machine.

The lonely starless April night
Swept the weather deck

Clean. The Gulf of Finland groaned
Under the icebreaker's sense

Of spring. At dawn we
Docked in a dogged

City dragged on by
Peter's horse:

Its copper tongue cracking
As it said, *Here*

there are more
museums, посетитель,

than your soft human
body has bones.

STOCKHOLM

Spring was the hammer
That fell down on Stockholm.

Grounded, the gray shattered.
Gamla stan greened.

The faint sound of the bay Riddarfjärden
Rose and fell, rose and fell

Like a dog asleep on its back
As pinkish dreamed demonstrations of place

Picked up their pieces
To put them back together again.

This was not all of Sweden, of course.
But sea-shouldered, mirroring, to itself

It thought to be so.
Like a boat in the distance

That thinks you are the distance.
And not itself. Not it.

For it is the center of everything.

TWO STUDIES OF DEREK WALCOTT

1.0: LEMON

This essay, its ten words for syllables, line by line
Succumbs to its paragraphic weight, as one by one eight
Gather over their ninth life, its twelve occasions mythwork like
Months to a mayfly. Edmund Spenser's house of exile aches.
Midway comes the idea that a palm frond's a page,
Each hem of the sea a quotation mark, the mind
(On the mend from itself, mending itself) a New Nation
Like New York, New London, maybe New Paltz; peelingly
    beautiful: a lemon rind
Quizzing the permanence of its tabletop, as an opened tulip
    does dirt.

2.0: NEPTUNE

The sea is blue, the sea is green, the sea
Is yellow when the sea is both sea and sun.
It erases. The seasons erase. A mirror erases its subject
And asks the vanished subject to love itself whole again.
Great, skymaking shepherd. Allegorist and allegory. What did
    you begin

With painted birds dotting your painted island in curatorial
    iambics;
And then the length, the length, the length: your ambition
Strong like Spenser's, who politicked in Ireland, while
    courting epic,
And caged his dark exilic woe behind lines burned black and
    lambent?

AUBADE: JARDINS DE WALTER BENJAMIN

4:59 in the morning
Is the color of shimmer
On a wet raven's shoulder.
Barcelona looms like a gondola
At the brim of the Muslim lake
Where plumed, perfumed palimpsests of
Wasp-waisted clubbers shine:
Some snow fed and fiddled with;
Some searching their cells for significance

As still in ties, still cardiganed, still propped by canes,
Under the half-light of a nearby park,
A small gathering of old men
Argues near their kiosk.
One of them curses in Catalan the shrapnel
Deep in his hip
That gave him when he was nineteen what age wouldn't:
His limp. He rubs it and rubs it and rubs it and
Rubs it and rubs it and rubs it and rubs it

As the sky unfolds to purple
Then bleeds quickly to red.
Long live the Republic.
The Republic is dead.

AUBADE, VOL. 2:

THE UNDERGROUND SESSIONS

The sun is a sequence of flash and din
In the sunken club's slanted black ceilings.
And where once the crowds were mere pent peacocks,
Twiddling half chatoyances, shimmers in the dark,
Now only the dancers remain.
The DJ rubs the mood of the room as though it
Were his womb. We dance: we ripple in place.
The twin black lakes of vinyl blend
Stirred to life by the dipped needle.

No one I know knows the real ends of when. (What?)
No one I know knows the real end of when. (What?)
No one I know knows for real when to end. Again.

No one I know knows for real when to end. (What?)
No one I know knows the real end of when. (What?)
No one I know knows the real ends of when.

And when we thought we'd reached the end
It was remixed again.
No one I know knows for real when to end.

As when a drinking collared deer
Hears a noise and
Although safe by being Caesar's
Feels a strange freedom there in that second,
Some sense in the gut, a thunder of ribs,
A surge in the blood, some cinched memory
Of not being Caesar's,

I change in the sameness of change.
I embrace the night and get gone.

SHEEP MEADOW

The same motion used
To make angels in the snow,
When standing
Is a signal of distress:
A frantic wave of the shipwrecked
To a distant, passing savior.

This angel in the snow.
This bent note blended into
The song of the snow.
The winter wind blowing
With the downbeat of the snow.

I fell backwards into it
And began that awkward grace,
But the ground wouldn't open.
I had to dig my way in.

And on my back I can see sharpen
The livid arch of the sky,
Hear it laugh at
The elusive horizon

Of the curving world;
Its ancient anchor slowly lifting
The ground adrift and absorbed.

En el blanco infinito
¡Qué pura y larga herida
Dejó su fantasia!
Lorca whispered to me
From a ditch
He can't climb out of,
As though I were born
In the calamitous balm of his mind.
But I was born in the bare choir
Of my own cold calor,
Where the snow silences the traffic
And the traffic silences the snow
As though nothing's left to describe,
No silence left to defile,
The sky said not saying,
The ground scrawling my name
Like a body scrawls an angel into the snow
Without the features of a face.

I get up from the ground
And take a look at what I've left:

Three triangles converging at a circle,
As if pointing to a head,
A head no one will know was my head.
The snow or the heat or someone's quick boot
Will put an end to that.
The snow, the forms,
They come and go,
Our parts in the world will come and go
Like limbs fading in the snow
While holding up a filling lake,
Its simple, imperfect circle
Orbiting the risen thought
That sang up to the atrament
Where the far-off instrument
Of the god of poetry
Waited to be played.

CLOSING NIGHT'S NOCTURNE

At the end of an excellent career
The moon combs her hair
For one final time
In the narrow half-lit window.

Tomorrow all her
Memorized lines
And muttered perfections,
All of her heights will burn.

Nothing left but the lights
That for so long framed the face,
And then, too, slowly the lights
To cinder.

Wait for the curtain to rise
Again. "The hours," she said.
"The hours I have now."
Wait for the encore.

Wait for the human bow.

HELL GATE, EAST RIVER, NEW YORK

Over the shorter shoulder of Manhattan,
Under gilded malts and molten-gold clouds, birds,
Lowering, seen as they were, lit by first light

And therefore first lit, dazzling the upper
Atmosphere, which, confused, fumed to dusk
As though perpetual, unctuous twilight

Was what was asked of it; under the gaudy matte,
With its tripled bridges, run-on projects, cellophane
High-rises, the sparse highway traffic accretive

Like a constellation, the September air
Grinding dawn down to one late summer moment
Far from the Hudson's twin songs of twilight

And daylight and was, where everything ever felt
Was thought to have fallen into that river,
Which made the river rise and fall with assured

Surfaces, surfaces smooth enough for
Apollo to pour his poems on and be glad;
Far from this; under the east's conversion,

Near the black island's old and tongueless lighthouse
That forks the East River's passage to the ocean
And makes where there was once one current

Thousands of circling currents, circling
Under red and chrome-colored arcs, currents
Swallowing themselves simultaneously, as

Though each is the pill that cures the other,
The long Dutch error crushed on a city's tongue,
Hellegat ground down into the smoldering pit;

Under what's real in it; under its faux-Dutch name;
Come the complications, *l'etterno dolore,*
Per me si va tra la perduta gente,

And those whom no house nor temple can contain.

THE END OF HIS LITTLE BOOK

Thus ends the story of that brave
And spirited poet,
Knave and ephebe of the city.

This book was translated
From Antiguan into Catalan
And thence into American

By that brave and
Magnificent knight
Sir Roland Barbaro Burns

Who, due to his untimely death,
Was unable to complete his task.
Thus, the last fourth was finished

(At the request of that noble lady whose name
Has been withheld at the bequest
Of her own benevolence)

By the brilliantly confused
Troubadour of unconfirmed descent,
Rowan Ricardo Phillips.

Therefore, should herein be found
Any faults
He hopes they will be attributed to ignorance

And prays Our Lord,
Whose name Is holy,
in His infinite munificence,

To reward him for his labors
With the glory
Of Paradise.

And likewise,
Should anything
Uncatholic

Be found in this book,
He shall rue the day
He wrote it

And submit it
For the ground's
Correction.

ACKNOWLEDGMENTS

Grateful acknowledgment is made to the following magazines and journals in which poems in this book first appeared, sometimes in slightly different form:

Callaloo: "*Purgatorio* XXVI: 135–148"
(as "Complex 26: Lost at Sea"), "Two Studies of
Derek Walcott" (as "Tableau: Derek Walcott")

Chelsea: "Map, Incomplete, 1665"
(as "Map, Incomplete, 1660"), "Eurydice"

Granta: "Abingdon Square Park," "Bird of Fire,"
"Reverse Eurydice," "Apollo: Season Three"

The Iowa Review: "Embrace the Night
and Get Thee Gone" (as "Echo")

jubilat: "Sonnet 3.0"

The New Republic: "Tonight," "A Vision Through the Smoke,"
"Mare Incognitum," "Closing Night's Nocturne"

The New Yorker: "Golden"

No: A Journal of the Arts: "Song of Fulton
and Gold" (as "Lower Quartet")

The Paris Review: "Heralds of Delicioso
Coco Helado," "Over the Counties of Kings
and Queens Came the Second Idea"

The Raintown Review: "Music for When the Music Is Over," "Two Twilights"

Seneca Review: "Sheep Meadow" (as "La Angelita Necesita . . .")

The Southampton Review: "Copper Horse," "Stockholm" (as "Skägård")

Tuesday; An Art Project: "Grief and the Imaginary Grave," "The Greenness of the Ground" (as "The Greenness of the Earth"), "Grief and the Imaginary Grave, Vol. 2: Red Trillium"